Getting to A+

Breakthrough Study Skills for High School Students

Written By: Kirsten Curtis

Cover Designed By: Marcus Dallas

To every high school student

who wants to do better in

school but is not sure how

Acknowledgments

This book would not have been possible without the support of my friends and family. I would first like to thank my father, Paul Curtis, who ignited the flame of inspiration inside me by waving his arms and shrieking, "Write, write, write. If you're going to be an author, write!!!" His admiration for my study habits was seminal in my decision to write this book. I have been infected by my father's contagious enthusiasm for story telling, and have adopted his tone and liveliness in my writing.

Secondly, I would like to thank Michael Zakaras, a dear friend of mine from Stanford University. The excitement he portrayed when describing his father's work made me enthusiastic about penning a book. He convinced me that writing was not something just for scholars, but for anyone who has an interesting story to tell.

Tanya Alexander and Phoebe Prioleau always seemed to ask me how my book was coming along two minutes before I was about to scrap the whole thing. Their support and encouragement helped me throughout the process.

Molly Meyer's presence can be felt throughout this book. She served as my inspiration, my source for outlandish, comical stories, and my chocolate delivery service when I needed a little pick-me-up. Molly saw to it that I finished my book before graduating from Stanford, devising a bet (which I lost!) to write three chapters over Christmas break.

Wendy Goldberg and Kalina Lowery edited my book, wading through my atrocious spelling and inappropriately used prepositions. I am extremely grateful for their time and suggestions.

I would also like to give a special thanks to Matt Gamboa, Stephanie Adams, Edward Boenig, Tess Williams, Molly Meyer, Will McLennen, Kent Anderson, Marisa Macias, Allison Campbell, Andy Clavin, Michael Zakaras, LaCona Woltmon, Jess Lang, and Emily Neaville for submitting their study skills.

Marcus Dallas spent countless hours designing the cover for this book. I am deeply grateful for all of the effort he put into this project.

A special thanks to Larry Rotter for proof-reading this manuscript and to Bill Ackerman for his technical assistance.

Finally, I would like to thank every single teacher I've had for helping me create my study skills. A special thanks to Mme. Pearlman and Ms. Lucchesi, who worked especially hard to shape my study habits, and who opened themselves up to me, enabling me to see their beautiful, fascinating personalities.

TABLE OF CONTENTS

Introduction

Nothing in the world can take the place of persistence. Talent will not; nothing is more common than unsuccessful men with talent. Genius will not; unrewarded genius is almost a proverb. Education will not; the world is full of educated derelicts. Persistence and determination alone are omnipotent.

~Calvin Coolidge

How can you do better in school? Intelligence and a good memory help, but study skills, persistence, and dedication constitute the foundation needed to get to A+. This might be a disappointment for those of you who were hoping for a magic potion to improve your GPA. Well, this recipe for success consists of hard work, commitment, and a basic knowledge of how the system works.

I base my opinion on personal experience. The fact of the matter is, I'm not that intelligent. (I once thought the word "golf" was spelled "golph." That was when I was 20.) My best friends are constantly saying, "You're really not that bright, are you?" And they're right; truth be told, I'm not the sharpest tool in the shed. But in spite of my mental capacity, I graduated high school Valedictorian with a 4.47 GPA, received academic scholarships, and graduated Phi Beta Kappa from Stanford University, maintaining a 3.9 GPA. I then went on to get my Master's of Engineering from MIT-Zaragoza (a partnership between MIT and the government of Spain) and graduated at the top of my class.

How is it possible that I, the "golpher," achieved this standing? I attribute my success to the study habits and techniques outlined in this book. My goal is to share with you the elements that allowed me to succeed. I am constantly refining my techniques, and you need not limit yourself to them. You may find some techniques that better suit your personality or lifestyle, and that's OK. These strategies have worked for me in the past, and I'm certain I wouldn't be where I am today without them. I hope even if these methods don't work out for you exactly the same way they have for me, they can at least get you on the path to success by enabling you to explore ways that work better for you. Most importantly, I want to convey the message that you can get to A+, even if you, too, are a "golpher."

1

In the Classroom

After a fellow gets famous it does not take long for someone to bob up that used to sit next to him in school.

~Kin Hubbard

Take Your Seats

It was the first day of the ninth grade. "Find a chair and sit down," Mr. Collins, the teacher, told me. I looked around the classroom like a wild animal backed into a corner, frantically scanning to the left and right, hoping an escape might present itself at just the right moment. Each one of the thirty-two empty chairs seemed to beckon me, and I was trapped in my indecision. Which one should I choose? Then, like a beam of light coming down from above, the answer unfolded: front row, center.

If you want to get the same grades as the smart kids, you have to give your teacher the impression that you're one of them. Sitting in the front row is one of the best ways to do that. Now, I don't mean to say that every single intelligent person sits in the front row. I've seen plenty of brains in the back of the class. But from my experience, the students in the front usually get good grades.

There are several reasons that can explain why students who sit in the front row have a greater chance of getting better grades. Perhaps the most important one is the false notion that the front row is reserved for A-students. Stereotypically, the students who get A's usually sit in the front row, but that doesn't mean that B or C students can't. More likely than not, though, the teacher and the class will assume that if you're in the front row, you must be smart.

Whether this perception is true or not, there are some definite advantages to sitting in the front row. First of all, the students in the front get the best view of the teacher, board, and overhead projector. I can't tell you the number of times I've seen people in the back squinting to see the board or straining to hear the teacher. I figure it's hard enough to learn the material the teacher is trying to get across. When you combine the challenge of understanding the curriculum with that of trying to see or hear, the task becomes overbearing, and it's just too easy to tune out.

This brings me to the next reason for why it pays to sit in the front. Because the front row is closer to the teacher, the students who sit there are inclined to be more accountable.

Get in the Habit of Sitting in the Front of the Classroom Now, and it will Pay off Even Bigger in College

The importance of sitting in the front row really became apparent in college. During my sophomore year at Stanford, I walked into a lecture hall with a friend who easily could have passed for a Greek God—rippling muscles, sun bleached hair, ocean-blue eyes, perfectly tanned skin. "Where do you want to sit?" he asked me in a voice that could have melted steel. I told him I usually sit in the front, and would he like to join me there? "Nah, I don't like to sit in the front. I can't fall asleep when I'm that close to the teacher." This was an interesting point. My friend went to class to fall asleep. We sat in the back row that day. (That's how I know it's hard to see from the back.) School was more important to me than drooling over this guy, though, so the next day I returned to the front and ended up doing much better than him in the class.

I mentioned before that sitting in the front row allows the best view of the teacher. If you have a really ugly teacher, this might seem like a drawback. However, ugly or not, it's important to remember this person (or creature, in some cases) is in charge of your grade. We'll get into how to deal with teachers later, but for now, let it suffice to say it's of the utmost importance to look your teacher in the eye and make sure she knows exactly who you are, and that she understands you're ready to learn whatever she might be teaching that day.

While this might seem somewhat ridiculous (are teachers really going to care where I sit?), it is important to remember what happens when grade time rolls around. Some teachers (especially math and science teachers) go by exactly how you did on the test (an 89.999 is still a B+,) but most teachers, particularly in the humanities, grade somewhat more subjectively. When deciding your grade, they look back and think, "Suzy was in the front, looking at me, and paying attention every day. She must be a good student; I should give her a good grade." It's as simple as that. I can't tell you the number of times teachers have pulled me aside at report-card time and said, "Your grade is an 87.6, which means an A-."

Advantages to Sitting in the Front of the Classroom

- There is a false notion that the front row is reserved for A-students
- You get the best view of the teacher/board/ overhead projector
- Proximity to the teacher increases your accountability
- You're in the perfect location to look the teacher in the eye and let him/her know that you're ready to learn!

But sitting in a prime location (i.e., the front, front-center if you can) does not guarantee your success in a class. It's a great start, but there's more to it than that. The image you give off is vastly important to getting good grades. I don't care how smart you are; if a teacher thinks you're a troublemaker, Smart-Aleck, or Chatty-Kathy, then it's going to be much more difficult for you to get top grades. But if you radiate the image of a motivated scholar or eager student, you are much more likely to receive favorable grades.

Creating the A-Student Image

So how do you create that A-student image? The first thing you can do is dress sharply for the first week of school. If you look like you're dressed up for school, teachers and students are going to think you take your education seriously. And first impressions are the most important. So on the first day of class, it's a great idea to introduce yourself to the teacher. Make sure he knows just who you are. Teachers see this as a sign of self-confidence and assertiveness, and those two qualities can really get you far in the classroom.

Fake It 'Til You Make It

It may seem superficial that just coming to class prepared, dressing sharply, and looking your teacher in the eye will help you get better grades. In reality, though, these things make a big difference, not only in high school, but also in college and in the working world. There's an entire industry (books, consultants, corporate trainings) built around creating a successful image. If you learn how to do this now, you'll be way ahead of the game later on in life.

Another way to give both teachers and other students the impression you're smart is to answer all the questions you possibly can. For example, every time the teacher asks a question, and you know the answer, be the first to raise your hand. Even if you're not entirely sure of the answer, make an educated guess. Your enthusiasm and participation will garner respect from the teacher. Plus, if you answer enough questions, chances are, the teacher won't call on you when you don't raise your hand, because you speak out enough already. Teachers want to give the other kids a chance to talk in class. Result: you're in charge of which questions you get to answer.

This strategy works especially well when teachers throw off-the-wall questions out to the class. You know the ones. They're the out of the blue, "Johnny, how many signatures are on the Declaration of Independence?" questions. Well, Johnny doesn't know, and you don't know, and the only kid who does know is the geek in the front with the glasses sitting next to you. But the reason the geek wasn't called on was because the teacher knew he knew the correct answer. And the reason you weren't called on was because you speak out often enough. Plus, because you're sitting in the front, the teacher might have figured you knew the answer, too. In any case, Johnny has to admit that he doesn't know, and while you had no idea either, you never had to reveal you didn't know the answer. Your image is preserved.

Another great way to boost your image is by taking notes. In college everybody takes notes—it's no big deal. This is not the case in high school. By taking notes, you raise yourself up to the collegiate level.

There are some great benefits to taking notes on the first day. Not only do you look like a serious student (for the image), but also teachers usually say some worthwhile things on the first day of class. For example, they might outline their plans for the semester or discuss some main themes that will be covered throughout the year. If you know what the important points are from the beginning, you will be in a lot better shape when test-time comes around. Furthermore, teachers usually disclose some personal information, which you can use to initiate conversations and establish connections with them. From a 9th grade World History class, I wrote, "Mr. Collins—likes sports cars, we'll be doing lots of recording, grades on points." This information, although it might seem cryptic to you, actually helped me better understand the teacher, which impacted my final grade.

In order to become an A-student, you have to act like one. Be aware that certain mistakes can blow the top student image. Forgetting a pen, paper, textbook, or homework assignment is not what an A-student does. This doesn't mean that if you forgot your book one time, you're never going to get an A. We all make mistakes, even the geek in the front with the glasses. But if you forget your materials often, you have a higher chance of blowing the A-student image. Therefore, it is very important to make sure you have all the necessary materials for a class. There are a few safety checks that you can to do to ensure you have all your stuff—from your biology textbook to a sharpened pencil.

First of all, organization is key. Keep a clean locker, a tidy backpack, and an organized desk. Having little scraps of paper creeping out of your binder, or turning in dog-eared homework, is not very professional. And that's how you have to think of school—it's your profession, and you need to do a good job if you want it to pay off. For that reason, it's always important to arrive on time, or even a little early. Leave yourself plenty of time to get to class.

If you have lots of time to get to class, you can take a minute to review the contents of your bag. Check to make sure you have a pen, paper, binder, book, and all those other nagging items teachers seem to demand of their students. Even if you forgot something, if you arrive to class early enough, you should have time to run back and grab it.

Locker Checklist: Don't Leave to Class Without . . .

☐ Sharpened Pencil

☐ Pen

☐ Binder Paper

☐ Correct Textbook

☐ Correct Binder/Notebook

☐ Homework

☐ Anything else you were supposed to bring

In the event that you do forget something, and you can't run back to your locker to get it, the best thing is to inform your teacher before class starts (which you should be able to do because you arrived early.) Tell her you forgot, for example, your Spanish workbook, and ask politely if you could please share with Tommy. Present a solution to your teacher (in this case, sharing with Tommy.) Teachers aren't unreasonable people, although I know sometimes it may seem that way. They have forgotten things in their life, too, and they'll understand if you've forgotten something (provided it doesn't happen often), you tell them about it before they ask you for it, and you present a solution on how to work around the problem.

Just as forgetting materials can blow the A-student image, leaving class can be a red flag to your teacher that you're not an A-student. But let's face it, sometimes you need to leave class to go to the bathroom. When this happens, ask the teacher if you can be excused.

Every teacher has his own policy on the number of times a student can leave class, and, as if that's not complicated enough, there're usually a few guidelines as to how a student must leave the classroom. (Can you just get up? Do you need to ask for permission? Does the teacher make you haul a toilet plunger with you, or is a hall pass sufficient?) Usually, these rules are disclosed on the first day of class—when you're taking notes—so be sure to pay attention to your specific teacher's policy. When in doubt about your teacher's preference, ask if you can go. This gives the teacher a sense of empowerment, which he generally likes to have. Don't dilly-dally in the hallways—return to class as soon as possible. Getting caught wandering the halls could get you in trouble and completely blow the A-student image. Now, you should really try to go to the bathroom during passing periods, breaks, or lunch. Don't get in the habit of leaving class at 10:10 every day to go pee. But once in a while, it's OK.

Creating the A-Student Image

- Dress sharply on the first day of class
- Introduce yourself to the teacher on the first day of class
- Take notes on the first day of class
- Sit in the front row
- Answer every question you possibly can
- Come to class prepared (make sure you look over your locker checklist)
- Arrive to class early, or at least on time
- Only leave class when absolutely necessary

In conclusion, in the classroom, it's important to maintain the image of an A-student, even if you're not yet one. Sit in the front of the class, preferably front-center. Look the teacher in the eye to let her know that you're there. Separate yourself from the other students by taking notes on the first day of class. Answer all the questions you can so you won't be called on randomly when the teacher asks really hard questions. Be sure to come to class prepared. Be accountable. Don't leave unless it's an emergency.

These techniques, if followed properly, will give you the A-student reputation needed in order for everybody but the geek with the glasses to get to A+.

Chapter 1 Summary Questions

1.) Where does the author recommend sitting?
   List three reasons why.

2.) What do you do when you know you've
   forgotten you homework at home? When
   you've forgotten a textbook?

3.) List six components of the A-student
   image.

4.) How are you going to incorporate what
   you've learned in this chapter into your
   classroom?

2

Managing Teachers

No man can be a good teacher unless he has feelings of warm affection toward his pupils and a genuine desire to impart to them what he himself believes to be of value.

~ Bertrand Russell

Whoever cares to learn will always find a teacher.

~ German Proverb

You don't have to think too hard when you talk to teachers.

~ J. D. Salinger

"She's a witch!" he blurted out. "More of a Nazi," the girl he was talking to contested. You know the type of teacher these students are describing. They're mean, heartless, crazy people. There have been times in my life when I wondered where these teachers came from:

29

hell or a loony house. Even now, as an adult, I'll walk into a class and shudder in the presence of some. But as I grew up, I began to understand that teachers, as unfair, cruel, and rotten as they may seem, are actually real people. While this concept might at first be difficult to wrap your head around, it's true! The hellish teacher teaching you math is a human deep down inside. She cries, laughs, and is capable of feeling a broad range of emotions.

Here's a little secret that took me a while to understand: teachers don't get paid very much. This means that they teach because they love to see the light go on in the eyes of their students. They feel like they're bettering the world by helping students. Of course, this idealistic image becomes tainted by the trouble-students: teachers constantly fighting with them, forcing them to learn, cramming information down their throats, only to have it be regurgitated in their faces. Naturally, this process isn't very fun and can embitter even the most optimistic teacher.

As a student, I've always thought it my job to rekindle the idea in the teacher's head that it's possible to improve the world by teaching me. This requires a certain amount of jumping through hoops. I've often struggled with this dilemma. Part of me doesn't want to have anything to do with the teacher—why am I responsible for bringing to life some dream he had years ago? But the other part of me knows that in life I am going to have to know how to relate to people— to empower them—and this skill will in turn benefit me. For this reason, I've diligently tried to be the dream of my teachers. And it has paid off, both in terms of my GPA and the relationships I've established with certain teachers. In the process of transforming myself into my teacher's dream, I've met some truly fascinating people. Under their thick skin, most teachers are wonderful people who've served to better my life. Bonding with teachers can really be a win-win process.

Creating a Rapport

The difference between establishing a rapport with teachers and sucking up or brown-nosing is very important. Teachers know a suck-up when they see one, and so do all the other students. And frankly, suck-ups aren't popular with either group. The best way to get around this issue is to convince the teacher, and yourself, that you are sincerely interested in learning. You want to learn it all. Whatever it is, they know a lot about it, and you don't, and you'd like to change that.

As we talked about in Chapter 1, sitting in the front of the classroom is very important, because it helps you pay attention to what is going on, and it makes you look like a smart kid. Use your strategic position to further that image. Nod your head at what the teacher is saying when you understand the concept being taught. As I mentioned before, teachers are humans, and at times they wonder if they are getting through to anybody. There's nothing worse for a teacher than staring into a crowd of blank faces. Nodding your head is like a beacon in the night. "Yes, somebody understands what I'm saying!" This will make the teacher feel reassured, and you are the one who got him to feel that way. Kudos to you.

If, however, you do not understand an issue, ask. Smart people ask questions. The worst thing you can do is stew in your own ignorance. That said, there comes a point when asking too many questions is annoying to the teacher and the other students. So ask, for example, your three most burning questions, and write the other ones down. (We'll be using those later.) Asking questions will help you, because you'll better understand the material being taught, and it will reassure the teacher that someone (that would be you) is paying attention and cares enough to ask about the unclear aspects of the subject matter.

Asking questions reassures the teacher that she is getting through to students, which makes her feel really happy. But there is another trick you can do to make teachers feel happy. As I mentioned before, teaching is a pretty thankless job: kids screaming, fighting, not paying attention—it can be a nightmare. This kind of life would make anyone cranky.

But there is something you can do to break the cycle—SMILE! Teachers love a smiling face. I find that smiling, in general, brings happiness. The effects are amplified for a teacher's rough job. So smile when you walk into the classroom. I once had an Italian professor who told me that a student who smiled in class made his job enjoyable. Did you ever think that you could make or break your teacher's day, just by smiling? Of course, teachers can make or break your GPA. I'd give smiling a try.

Fueling the Dream

- Convince yourself, as well as your teacher, that you sincerely want to learn
- Communicate with your teacher by nodding your head when you understand
- Ask questions when something is unclear
- Smile
- Acknowledge a teacher's presence outside the classroom
- Make time to get together with your teacher after class

It's necessary to remember your relationship with your teacher extends beyond the classroom. This is a concept not many students understand. Teachers, although they seem like a species of their own, really are normal people. If you saw your mom's friend in the supermarket, what would you do? Turn down your eyes, make a face, and whisper "witch" under your breath? I hardly think so. Normal people don't deserve this kind of reaction, and teachers don't either. When you see a teacher in the hall, or around the town, say hello. Even if you don't like the teacher, it shows strength of character, and it will help you get what you want.

Working with People You Don't Like

In business, the odds are that at some point in your career you'll have to work with someone you don't like. This may be a colleague, a boss, or a subordinate. Even if this person is a total train wreck, your inability to work with him will reflect negatively on you. In order for you to be successful, you will have to learn how to work with this person. If you can figure out now how to work with disasters, you will have acquired a skill that will serve you later on in life.

At the bare minimum, you need to treat a teacher like any other adult. But if you feel so inclined, you can treat your teacher as a mentor, or even as a friend. I don't know if anything is more flattering than having someone admire you. If you look up to certain teachers, let them know.

CAUTION: Don't pretend you admire a teacher when you really don't. It would be a mistake to tell a teacher who has a voice like a frog that you love to hear her speak, because her words sound as soothing as a lullaby. This would be sucking up, and everyone can see through that. Talk to your teachers before or after class, or whenever they are free. (Do make sure that they have time; otherwise you may be perceived as a pest.) Teachers, oftentimes, know a lot of cool stuff.

> **DON'T PRETEND YOU ADMIRE A**
>
> **TEACHER IF YOU DON'T!**

I once had coffee with an English professor. This woman was awesome! She told me about all this really cool research that was going on with language, and how some philosophers believe that ideas are created through language. It was really fascinating. I

Office Hour Etiquette

- Don't wait until the last minute to make an appointment
- Arrange a convenient time to meet with your teacher
- Be sure to show up to the meeting on time
- Come prepared with questions
- Thank your teacher for meeting with you

Contesting a Grade

In your academic career, it's possible that you'll get a grade you think is unfair or undeserved. While teachers usually try to be as fair as possible, sometimes they make mistakes. My best friend's father was a professor at a university. He told me he would grade papers in the living room after dinner. Once in a while, my best friend would sit with his father while he read numerous essays. My friend told me whenever his father would give a B- to someone, he would feel sorry for the student and say, "Come on,

Dad, be nice." His father (and this is what really gets me), would look at my friend, and then say, "OK, you're right. I'll be nice," and change the grade to a B+. Can you even believe that this sort of thing happens? Maybe your teacher has a kid at home who says, "Come on, Mom, be mean. That's not a B-paper. It deserves a C."

If you feel your grade is unjust, the best way to deal with it is to schedule a meeting with your teacher. At the meeting, it is crucial to say, "Mr. Strong, I got a C on this paper, and I'm curious as to why. Could you please explain to me how you evaluated the assignment?" Asking the teacher to justify your grade is a far better technique than asking him to bump up your grade.

You see, if you walk into a meeting, and start the conversation off with, "I got a C and I should have gotten an A. You need to change my grade," the teacher goes on the defensive. Inside his head, he's thinking, "No, I won't change your grade. If you got a C, then that's what you deserve." By offering the teacher only one option (to change your grade), you put the teacher in a position to refute your request.

However, if you ask your teacher to justify his strategy, he will have to look back through the paper, and in doing so he might realize what you did wasn't so bad after all. It's like you get to have your paper graded a second time.

In a political science class I took at Stanford, I got a B+ on a midterm paper. While most people might be happy with a B+, I was devastated. I had put so much work into that paper, and I thought it could've well been the best piece of work I had ever churned out. And the T.A. had given me a B+.

I made an appointment with the aforementioned T.A. and asked her why I got the grade I did. She said what she was looking for in the paper was some sort of historical analysis, blah, blah, blah. "Like on page 18?" I questioned. She reread the page, and said, "Yes, that's right. But you didn't do this, that, and the other thing." I told her to look at specific sections, and it turns out I did a pretty good job of writing about whatever it was she was looking for. "Well, I guess you did do a pretty good job," she confessed after going through my paper again. I'll give you an A-."

The order in which you go about negotiating a grade change is very important. Below are the steps.

Grade Changing Sequence

1.) Set up an appointment with the teacher to "talk" about the assignment. Say that you have some "questions"

2.) Start the session by saying, "I got a 'C' on this paper, and I would like to know what I can do to better my performance in the future"

3.) Listen to what the teacher has to say

4.) If you did some of those things, point them out

5.) LISTEN to what you **didn't** do, but should have done

6.) If your work turned out to be better than once thought by the teacher, let her suggest a grade change

7.) If your work wasn't what she was looking for, make sure you understand how to make it better in the future

8.) Be sure to thank the teacher for her time

Remember, don't even bother contesting a grade unless you feel you truly deserve a better one.

Chapter 2 Summary Questions

1.) What does the author really think about teachers?

2.) What are some things you can do to establish a good relationship with a teacher?

3.) What are office hours? What should you do to prepare for office hours?

4.) Are you going to try any of these techniques? Which ones? How are they going to fit into your everyday routine?

3

Overcoming Assigned Reading

*To acquire the habit of reading is to
construct for yourself a refuge from
almost all of the miseries of life.*

> *~W. Somerset Maugham*

*Force yourself to reflect on what you
read, paragraph by paragraph.*

> *~Samuel Taylor Coleridge*

*I must say that I find television very
educational. The minute somebody turns
it on, I go to the library and read a book.*

> *~ Groucho Marx*

In my experience, the amount of time you put into reading a book equals the amount of value you will get out of it. It becomes a question of time management and how hard you want to work. If you're willing to go all the way, you can really get a lot out of the books you read. In this section I'll describe the super-star way of reading, but you can alter the method if you're short on time.

Beyond the Assigned Pages

When reading was assigned in high school, I read the exact number of pages assigned, and not a word more. (Sometimes I wouldn't even look at the title of the chapter!) But this really got me into trouble in college, so I suggest you start forming good reading habits now. When opening a book, start at the beginning. Look through the table of contents. Read the introduction. The author wrote it for a reason. And here's the reason: more often than not, by reading the preface or the introduction, or breezing through the table of contents, you will get a feel for what's going to happen in the book.

Mark, a history T.A. at Stanford University, pointed this out to me. We were reading an obtuse book, and the chapters just seemed to be compiled in a mish-mosh sort of a way. We'd been assigned to write a paper on the author's thesis, and I couldn't even imagine what the point of the book was. I assumed it had something to do with history, since that was the subject of the class, but that was as close as I got.

As outlined in Chapter 2, I made an appointment with Mark to discuss the paper. Walking into Mark's office, I was in a panic, sweat oozing from my pores. How could I possibly write a paper on something I didn't understand at ALL! Mark began by choosing passages and having me look over them. We talked about these certain sections, but I had a feeling it was more to prove to him I had done the reading than to help me with the paper, because after about 20 minutes of chatting I still didn't know what the heck the thesis was.

Then Mark turned to me and asked, "Did you read the preface?" I had not. "Did you look at the table of contents?" Negative. Mark just shook his head and turned to the front of the book. We looked at the table of contents, and suddenly I saw a progression I hadn't noticed when just reading the chapters. The book was split into different time-periods that influenced each other. I didn't have the thesis yet, but I had a much better idea of how the book was laid out. Then Mark flipped to the preface. Right there, in black and white, the author had laid out his thesis. My face turned a bright pink, and I thanked Mark for his time and told him that I was off to write a paper.

Keep in mind the preface and the table of contents don't always hold the magical answer. You can use your own judgment to decide if reading the preface or the table of contents is valuable.

Interaction and Interrogation

Perhaps the most important aspect of reading is interacting with the book. You need to throw off the cloak of common perception that reading a book means just reading. If you want to do well, you need to do more than just read—you must take notes, ask questions, and write summaries. Reading a book is more like interviewing an author and then writing a newspaper article about his work. Interrogate the text!

First, you need to ask yourself questions like, "Why is this true? How come? Does this relate to the last chapter? How? Why did the author include that?

What is the significance of this? What are the implications? How does A affect B?" and so on.

A Sample of Questions to Ask When Reading:

- Why is this true?
- How come?
- Does this relate to the last chapter? How?
- Why did the author include this?
- What is the significance of that?
- How does A affect B?

It's not enough to just ask these questions in your head—write them in the margins. If you just ask the questions in your head, it's easy to forget them. "Well, I had a good question from a few chapters back, but I forgot what it was, so I won't worry about it now." NO! Write down the questions, and then write down the answers. If one of your questions didn't get answered by the author, earmark the page and ask your teacher about it.

I've done a lot of reading, and writing in a book is perhaps one of the most important parts of reading. First of all, it helps you stay awake. It's a lot harder to fall asleep when you're writing, versus when you're just reading. Plus, it makes reading a lot more interesting, because you're moving around physically, and you're mentally interacting. In addition, writing in a book makes reading more exciting, because you can pretend that you're interviewing the author instead of just reading a dumb book.

The value of taking notes in a book cannot be stressed enough, but sometimes it's difficult to know exactly what to take notes on. As mentioned, write your questions, and their answers, in the margins.

Furthermore, you should underline anything you think might be important. After reading the preface, you should have an idea of what you're looking for in the book, and you can underline any points that are part of the author's argument. What to underline depends somewhat on the kind of book you are reading. If it's a science book, you might want to underline exactly how something works. (The human body produces 36 ATPs in oxidative respiration.) Here is an example[i]:

Underline Key Points

More than <u>1.2 million people</u> die each year from malaria, most of them <u>children under the age of six.</u> The global community has recently awoken to the tremendous avoidable suffering caused by this disease, and today the fight against malaria is <u>garnering significant donor funds</u>. In <u>2002</u>, donors committed approximately <u>$200</u> million annually to fighting malaria. <u>Today,</u> that number is estimated at <u>$885</u> million and is projected to more than double over the next two years to almost $2 billion annually. In <u>a ten-year period, funding for malaria will increase ten-fold</u> - a dramatic scale-up by any standards.

If you're reading a novel, mark powerful, moving sentences or beautiful phrases. By and large, underline phrases you want to remember, you think are important, and and/or you want to refer back to.

What's Worth Underlining?

- Thesis
- Main point of a passage
- Powerful sentences
- Moving phrases
- Anything you might want to refer back to

The more you read, the more you'll realize what should be underlined. As a word of caution, though, avoid over-underlining. I was reading a fascinating scientific paper, and everything seemed important. I wanted to remember it all. So I underlined it all. "Boy, I'm getting some great interaction here. I'm really going to understand all this stuff," I thought to myself. But when I went back to reread the key points, the pages looked like this[ii]:

Example of Over-Underlining

A system with many independent <u>stakeholders, functioning in a loose network, works well in achieving its objectives if the incentives of all parties are aligned, towards a common goal</u>. In the case of ACTs this means that the <u>risks, costs, and rewards of doing business should be distributed fairly across the network towards the common goal of improved access.</u> Each stakeholder should have an explicit incentive to engage in activities that support the <u>goal of increased access.</u> ☆

<u>This is particularly critical in the complex and often confusing global health environment which consists of donors who are subject to a multitude of national political pressures; funders such as the Global Fund, who rely on annual funding rounds and must balance the conflicting objectives and political priorities of multiple donors; countries who don't pay directly for products but take multiple actions to get access to money and drugs; manufacturers who often sell their products at cost and therefore participate in the market more for public relations than for profits; and a host of technical agencies and</u> ☆ <u>intermediaries who play multiple, sometimes ill-defined roles in the value chain.</u> Access to treatments is further constrained by <u>dysfunctional country health systems</u> spending a few dollars per person on health care and delivering care to the poor and most vulnerable.

What a mess! There was no way I was going to reread the important points of that chapter, because I couldn't tell what was important. This is when I learned you need to be somewhat selective and underline only the most important points. To find the important points, it's a good idea to finish reading the sentence, or even paragraph, before you start underlining. You can put a star by the really important words, highlight essential phrases, use a red pen to note your questions, and make comments in the margins in pencil. Devise your own system of deciding what's important, what's really important, what you need to go back to look at, what you have questions on, what you have comments on, and what doesn't makes sense.

Symbols and Meanings

⌐......Check this part out
|...... Interesting points
☆.....Wow!
".......Look over this one
√......Yes, I get it!
?........What the hell?

In some books, the author gives you a chance to interact with the text by providing summary questions, certain vocabulary words, and key points at the end of the chapters. I urge you to read the key points, test yourself on the vocabulary, and answer—and I mean really answer—the summary questions. It's easy to get lazy and say to yourself, "Yah, I know what that means," or "Oh, I know the answer to that," but sometimes we don't know quite as much as we think we do. Other times, we understand a concept, but can't verbalize it.

By stepping back and really answering the questions or explaining certain concepts, as if you were a teacher, you get a much better idea of what you know and what you need to review. If you find that some points are a little fuzzy (in other words, you thought you could answer the question, but when you tried, you fumbled around and finally gave up,) go back and look up the answers in the book. Solidify your understanding.

Outline Review

Part of the reason to take notes in the margins is not only to interact with the book, but also to make it easier to go back and review. Before a test, and we'll get to this later, you'll want to review the most important points. What I like to do after every chapter is write a brief summary of the most important points. Here is an example of a chapter summary outline I wrote at the end of a chapter on the Cold War in a political science book:

End of Chapter Outline Example

Key Chapter Point: <u>Nixon and Kissinger: How much of the problem were they responsible for?</u>

I. Linkage Failed
- Moscow didn't buy into it. Preferred compartmentalized negotiations
- Failure of 3rd world countries: US & USSR didn't agree on what to do with them
- Russians had their own ideas

II. Military power
- Russians engaged in huge build up
- Military Spending: SALT Treaties come about; Russia has the advantage
- US doesn't build up and Russia does, giving Russia the advantage. NOT GOOD for U.S.

III. Kissinger oversimplifies problem
- Super Power Response or none at all
- Caused little crises to become global due to inability to deal with scale of problem

With summaries like this, you'll be able to go back quickly and review exactly what is in each chapter. Instead of rereading the entire book, you just have to look at the end of each chapter in order to refresh your memory. I like to write what the point of each page or section is. This way, when I make the summary, all I have to do is flip through the chapter, write down all the main points, and then see how they flow together.

You'll find by teasing out the main points, the book will become more comprehensible. If you understand what the author is trying to get across, you'll have an easier time remembering it.

Authors often write a main point and then reinforce it with examples, details, and anecdotes. If you can just get the main points out of a book, and not worry about the rest, you'll have a much easier time understanding the plot of the book and remembering its point. Then you can go to the examples or anecdotes for a specific reference. In other words, instead of trying to remember everything you read, distill the main points or arguments, understand them, and then choose one or two examples that reinforce them. The summary will enable you to do this, and it will free up your mind from all the details you would otherwise be trying to cram into your brain.

As a review: don't just read a book—interact with it! Write questions and comments in the margins. Ask your teacher about anything you don't understand. Mark important passages. At the end of each chapter, write a quick summary of what happened and why it's important. Distill the most important points the author is making, and be able to back those points up with a few specific examples. This type of reading will ensure you understand the book, which is the goal of reading in the first place!

Chapter 3 Summary Questions

1.) What does interacting with the text mean?

2.) What sort of things might you underline?

3.) What type of pen/pencil/highlighter do you like to use? What symbols do you find useful?

4.) What does the author suggest you do at the end of every chapter?

4

Mastering the Essay

Writing is exploration. You start from nothing and learn as you go.

~E.L. Doctorow

Writing is very easy. All you do is sit in front of a typewriter keyboard until little drops of blood appear on your forehead.

~Walter W. "Red" Smith

Writing is perhaps one of the most important ways we communicate our thoughts and ideas with others. Your writing is an expression of your soul—your feelings, views, values, and opinions are the building blocks upon which your words are built. Yet writing is hardly ever taught this way in school. For me at least, writing in high school had just about as much personal expression as taking out the garbage. Writing papers was a terrible part of my English education. I was always forced to write about mundane things in an expository style (Does anyone know what this is, anyway?), and I hated every minute of it. It wasn't until I met Professor Lisa Manter, one of my college English professors, that I learned writing is so much more than a five-paragraph essay. Writing can be fun and exciting, and if you're able to break free of the trite shackles that constrain your writing, your work will become interesting to write and fascinating to read.

Choosing Your Context

Before you start writing, figure out what kind of assignment you're supposed to be doing. Is it a creative writing assignment? A summary of a book? Or are you supposed to comment on a particular passage? Depending on the assignment, the style of your writing will vary. The diction and tone you use in your creative writing might be vastly different from what you would use in an academic paper. Some teachers call this the rhetorical situation. What that basically means is pairing up your writing assignment with its appropriate audience and purpose. In other words, just pay attention to what kind of paper is expected and who the audience is, and write accordingly.

If you're given a prompt (e.g., "Comment on the way Dickens uses hands in the following passage from *Great Expectations*,") your essay might already be fairly focused. But sometimes you will have to decide for yourself what you want to write about. My advice is to choose a topic that is narrow enough so you can be specific, but not too narrow, because you might have only one thing to say about it—which is a problem if you're supposed to write a five page paper.

"Commenting" De-Mystified

"Commenting" on a passage can be extremely difficult, specifically because it measures not only your writing capabilities but your reading ones, as well. Your ability to analyze a text depends on your ability to read it. One way to start an analysis is to consider the style an author uses. Is it unique in some way? How? Does the author use symbols, or metaphors, or allusions in his writing? If so, why? What are their effects? When writing about the passage, put it into the context of the work. Is this a seminal passage? Does it serve as an illustration of the author's thesis? What happens before the passage; what happens after? How does the passage add to the book as a whole?

Now, if you really want to blow your teacher's socks off, you can go into how this passage fits into the context of history. Figure out at what point in time the passage was written. Do a little research about what was going on during that time. Does history relate to what the author was writing about? If not, forget it. But just imagine if it did. Think about how totally amazed your teacher would be if you wrote, "Pierre Cadeau wrote this book during the end of the 19th century, a period in history noted for its colonial imperialism. The relation between the slave and his master could represent the political relationship between France and its colonies." Wow!

If you can't find any relationships between a book/passage and when it was written, pay attention to names. Shakespeare wrote, "What's in a name? That which we call a rose by any other name would smell as sweet," as an ironic way to highlight the importance of names. In *Romeo and Juliet*, names were the dividing force between the lovers. Often in literature names carry a great significance. Perform a web-search of any name that appears in the text. For instance, Hamlet was derived from the name of a Dutch prince and, therefore, carried a political meaning. In *Grapes of Wrath*, Steinbeck names the preacher Jim Casey, a man whose initials, J.C., carry religious significance. These are just a few examples of the way authors assign meaning to their characters' names.

You Could Comment on:

- Style
- Symbols
- Allusions
- Literary context
- Diction
- Metaphors
- Names
- Historical context

Decide what you want to focus on: the author's style, the way the piece fits into the context of the book, or even the larger context of history. When you have your topic narrowed down, make sure the size of your topic fits that of the assignment. For example, if you're asked to write one page, and you know you could write twenty pages on the way the passage fits into history, you might want to choose a different subject. In other words, don't try to cram twenty pages worth of writing into one page. Likewise, if you think you can go on for about a page and a half talking about the author's diction, don't use this topic for a twenty-page paper. You need to match the size of the paper to how much you think you can write about a particular subject. There's nothing worse than reading fluff for eighteen pages, because you said everything there was to say in the first two, or getting just a brief overview instead of any concrete examples, because there wasn't enough space. Use your best judgment here.

Courteous Writing

Once you have your topic narrowed down, you can focus on the writing part of the assignment. Perhaps one of the most important things to keep in mind when writing is the person reading it. Have you ever read a terrible book? Or something that you just didn't understand at all? Maybe it was a classmate's paper, containing nothing but sentence fragments, incomplete thoughts, and lacking organization *in toto*. The purpose of writing is communication. If your teacher, or anyone who is reading your work, can't understand what you're writing, what's the point?

Tailoring Your Message to the Audience

Being a courteous writer and keeping your audience in mind is a skill that will be very important when you enter the business world. A memo to a top executive will require bullet points and succinct sentences that will most likely fit on only one page, whereas an in-depth analysis of market segmentations may be 100 pages and contain charts, graphs, and more details than you can shake a stick at. Remembering who is intended to read your message will help you in making sure your message gets heard.

To keep the reader up to pace with your racing thoughts and ideas, you should follow some conventional procedures.

Organization Helps Communication

Your teacher, or any reader, is going to be looking for your thesis and the subject of each of your supporting paragraphs (or the road-map, as I like to call it) in the introduction. The opening begs for finesse; the ways you share your thesis and road-map are up to you. When I was in high school, my English teacher told me I needed to state my thesis and follow it up with the topics of my three supporting paragraphs. I found this extremely difficult, partially because I didn't know what the body of my paper was going to be about. I learned in college that wasn't a problem.

If you don't know what your paper is going to be about, that's OK. Whether you make an outline and then write the paper, or write the paper and then figure out how to organize it, is arbitrary. If you don't know how your paper is going to flow, and you're getting stuck on the introduction, just start writing. Write everything that comes to mind—all the points you want to make, all the quotes you want to include. Then go back and figure out the best way to organize your thoughts.

See if you can include some points with others, and pair up certain examples that go with particular points. Then, when you write your introduction, you'll know what you want to say. As a matter of fact, Molly, my roommate at Stanford, usually writes her paper and then writes her introduction. Molly's method can actually be better than writing an introduction right off the bat. She knows exactly what she's introducing. This means her thoughts are coherent, which the reader will really appreciate.

TRY WRITING YOUR PAPER AND THEN YOUR INTRODUCTION

From Beginning to End

The introduction and the conclusion are the two most important paragraphs of your paper. According to the book *Writing with Style*, "your opener is critical . . . [and has] a way of governing how the rest of the piece gets written."[iii] In the introduction, you need to grab your reader and bring her into your piece. After reading your opening paragraph, you want the reader to be so enthralled with your work that she can't put your paper down.

You have to grab the reader's interest and spark her curiosity. Opening sentences, fragments, and exclamations are great ways to seduce the reader. For example, I once started a paper with the sentence, "It happened on a Thursday." Immediately, the reader is wondering what happened. She wants to find out. So she keeps reading the paper. Your introduction should be a carrot in front of the reader's nose. Give her just enough information to keep her interested, and dangle that carrot in front of her until the conclusion.

Introduction Seduction

- Catch phrase to start things off
- Thesis
- Road-map
- Finessed, flowing sentences to keep the reader enthralled

This brings me to my next topic: the conclusion. Like the introduction, the conclusion is extremely important. The conclusion is the last part of the paper your reader is going to look at, and is, therefore, your final chance to leave a lasting impression. There are some conventionalities that should be included in a conclusion. First of all, you should summarize your points. Briefly, in a sentence or two, remind the reader what your paper was about, and how you proved your points. Make sure your conclusion answers the "so what?" question. This will provide your paper with closure.

But then, leave the reader with something to think about. Like the catch phrase you used in the introduction, the last sentence of your paper should suggest something that will become seared into the reader's mind. It could be a new twist on the points you were making, a question, or some sort of implication.

Now here's where we draw a fine line. You want to leave the reader with something a little different, but you don't want it to be so different that it doesn't fit into the subject of the paper at all or contradict your thesis. For example, if you were writing about your trip to Alaska, and you talked about skiing, going to bars, and meeting all sorts of mountaineers, you wouldn't want your last sentence to be, "With all these people, does anyone think of the environmental impact on polar bears?" Although there are polar bears in Alaska, what do they have to do with your trip there?

A better ending would be, "While most people think of Alaska as a desolate country inhabited by wolves and polar bears, my experience has shown there are recreational activities and fun loving people there. Goodbye, New York City. Hello, Anchorage!" This ending includes a brief reiteration of the thesis (your trip to Alaska and what it was like), and the last phrase leads the reader to believe that you might be moving to Alaska based on your experience. Comparing Anchorage to New York City makes the reader really think about the points you made regarding Anchorage being populated and full of things to do.

When writing a conclusion, there are a few things you should avoid. First of all, steer clear from just fading out or just amassing all the left-over points and jamming them into one paragraph. I understand you might be tired of writing—maybe you're pushing a page limit quota, or perhaps you just want to finish the darn thing so you can go out and chill with your friends. But just ending your paper or filling the ending with left-overs isn't fair to the reader, and it's not fair to you, either. You've worked hard on this paper—give it the ending it deserves.

To Include, When You Conclude:

- Restatement of your thesis
- Reminder of what your points were and how you proved them
- A new spin or idea that is going to imprint your last words on the reader's brain

---

Body Type

We have covered the elements of an introduction and a conclusion, but what about the body of your paper? My high school English teacher told me the body of the paper should support my thesis. But what does that mean? How can you support your thesis? And how can you make something like supporting a thesis interesting?

First, let's talk about conventionality. As in your introduction and conclusion, each paragraph in the body of your paper plays a particular role, and each paragraph should have a topic. Say you want to write about how a character in a book is really a symbol of former President George W. Bush. Begin by asking yourself, "How am I going to prove this point?" Perhaps you decide that the character's name, Mr. H. Sub, is Bush spelled backwards. This is an important point, and you might want to make it the topic of your first paragraph.

But just because the character's name is Bush spelled backwards, your reader might still not be convinced the character actually represents the former President. So, you need to bring in more evidence. The topic of your second paragraph might talk about the characteristics of Mr. H. Sub. Perhaps he is portrayed as a cowboy, whose goal is to bring freedom to everyone. Maybe Mr. H. Sub uses the words "liberate" or "democracy" in his rhetoric. Bring in quotes from the reading to show there are similarities between what Bush said during his presidential terms and what Mr. H. Sub talks about in the novel.

Finally, in your third paragraph you can talk about the time in which the book was written. Do a little research. Maybe the book was written in 2003 by a political activist who was avidly against the war in Iraq. Talk about the author's viewpoint and what he accomplished by portraying the former President as Mr. H. Sub.

Your body paragraphs need to flow together. A good way to do this is to make the opening sentence of one paragraph mention the topic of your last paragraph. For example, in our Bush illustration, an opening sentence for the second body paragraph might be, "Not only does the author portray Bush's similarities to Mr. H. Sub through his name, he also furthers his point by tapping into similarities between their personalities." This opening sentence is related to the first paragraph, and it also introduces the theme of the second paragraph. The reader is reminded about the point that was made in the first paragraph and is ready to read about how the two personalities are related.

The body paragraphs should include a statement and evidence to back up your point. Just as each body paragraph supports your thesis, there is going to be evidence in each body paragraph to support the theme of the paragraph. Let's stick with the second paragraph of the Bush example. You made your claim that Bush and Mr. H. Sub share similar personality characteristics. To prove this to the reader, use quotes.

Quoting

There are three things you need to do when you quote. First, you need to introduce the quote. Say what it is going to be about. For example, "Bush and Mr. H. Sub share a lot of similar personality characteristics." Now the reader knows what the quote is going to be about. Then lay in the quote. "For example, Mr. H. Sub is described as 'a daring cowboy, willing to fight for liberty and justice for all.'" Then you need to remind the reader how this quote proves your point. "Both men are described as being cowboys. Both are willing to fight for liberty and justice. The phrase 'liberty and justice for all' comes directly from the Pledge of Allegiance. The author is tapping into yet another similarity of American values that both characters share."

The analysis of your quote, or the way it proves your point, is where you get to shine. Really show the reader how well you read the passage/book and how well you understood its greater context. This is your chance to demonstrate how much work and thought you have put into your paper.

Quote Formula

- Introduce quote
- Quote
- Analyze quote

Quotes are a great way to bring textual evidence into your paper, but teachers often warn students not to over-quote. My first introduction to the idea of over-quoting came to me on a winter's day in my sophomore year of high school, when my English teacher warned the class that those who over-quoted would fail. I wasn't sure at the time what over-quoting was, but I avoided using quotes until well into my junior year, because I was so afraid of over-quoting. Then I learned what over-quoting meant.

Teachers want to hear what you have to say. Quotes are a great way to prove your points, but if you cram as many quotes onto a page as possible, the paper starts to resemble an opinions-page from some on-line forum instead of your work. Likewise, if you insert a page of what another author has written, you lose the tone of your own voice. As long as you tease out the essential part of a quote, and surround it with an introduction and an explanation of how this quote proves your point, you won't have to worry about over-quoting.

You now have the basic formula for how to write a paper. As a reminder, there is a recipe or formula that each reader will be looking for. Let's review:

Recipe for the Conventional Essay

Introduction:
- Get the reader's attention by using a catch phrase!
- Introduce the thesis
- Include the main points of the supporting paragraphs

First Paragraph:
- Introduce the topic and give examples
- Use quotes as evidence. Use quote formula: introduce quote, give the quote, and follow it up by explaining how it supports your point

Second Paragraph:
- Introduce the topic and try to relate the second paragraph to the main point of the first paragraph
- Use quotes and quote formula again

Third Paragraph:
- Introduce the topic and try to relate it to the topic of the second paragraph
- Use quotes and quote formula again

Conclusion:
- Reiterate your thesis
- Remind the reader about the topics of your three main paragraphs
- Give the reader a little something by which to remember you

Add Your Style

There you have it: the structure of an excellent paper. Now it's up to you to use your creativity to decide how you want to fill in the blanks. What examples do you want to use? How are you going to keep your writing style interesting? A tip I like to keep in mind is to vary my style. I like to use long sentences and then occasionally throw in a short one. Switch up the punctuation; use semi-colons here and there. Toss in an exclamation mark if you want to catch the reader's attention! Starting a sentence with a verb in the gerund tense can make it more exciting. Instead of using mundane words, like "nice" and "fun," consult a thesaurus for words that are not as common. Use metaphors, similes, and personification in your creative writing. Think about what you have learned in school when you were reading the works of different authors, and see if you can incorporate some of their style into your own writing. Be experimental when you can. Try to express yourself through your words.

Writing vs. Rewriting

When you have finished writing your paper, you can begin the long revision process. Someone once said that a finished text was actually only 10% writing and 90% re-writing. Revising is extremely useful and will help you become a strong writer. When I finish a paper, I like to take a little break, maybe for an hour, a day, or even a week depending on how much time I have. Then I like to pick up my paper and pretend that it is the work of my worst enemy. I pretend I'm supposed to edit this kid's paper, and you can believe I'm going to be as scrutinizing as possible. Red pen in hand, I begin marking up the paper as much as I can.

But what to look for? First, read through the paper and ask yourself, "Did I answer the question?" If a prompt was given, did you sufficiently respond to it? If no prompt was given, did you stick to your thesis? Then look at the structure of your paper. Did you follow the plan that you laid out in the introduction? Did you give a subject to each paragraph? (It helps to write what the subject is next to the paragraph so you can focus on it.) Did you provide enough supporting evidence? How well did you introduce and analyze the quotes? Did you catch the reader's attention in the introduction, and did you leave the reader with something to think about in the conclusion? Did you sum up your main points in the conclusion?

Don't be afraid to mark up your paper. As I mentioned, pretend it's someone else's paper. If the introduction doesn't grab your attention, cross it out. If the conclusion is weak, write: "You need to write a better conclusion. Get rid of this one!" If you don't like the examples used, write a note to find new ones. If something doesn't make sense, or if you don't like it, cross it out! Get rid of it! Don't try to salvage a weak part of your paper out of laziness. Your teacher will recognize the weak aspects and will take a pen to them. If you want a good grade, it's better that you do this yourself.

After analyzing the structure and paying close attention to how well the paper flows, look at the writing. Are there grammatical errors? Are there sentences that just don't make sense? Is some of the wording awkward? Read through each sentence and ask yourself, "Does this make sense? How do you know this? Where do you get this idea? Is there a better way to phrase this point? What exactly does this mean?" Again, be as critical as you can. At this point, you are not trying to fix your paper; you're just trying to find all the weaknesses in it. Mark now, and fix later.

Revising Checklist

- ☐ Answered the question
- ☐ Clearly stated thesis
- ☐ Had strong supporting paragraphs
- ☐ Incorporated textual evidence
- ☐ Effectively used quotes and quote formula
- ☐ Introduction grabbed the reader's attention
- ☐ Conclusion tied everything together
- ☐ No spelling mistakes
- ☐ No grammatical mistakes
- ☐ No awkward sentences/unclear phrases

When you finish marking up your paper, go back and fix your errors. Rewrite paragraphs, find better quotes, fix your spelling, and finesse your introduction. While this takes time, it will really help your paper. Once you have repaired your paper, let it sit for a few more days/hours. Then go back and, pretending it's once again your worst enemy's, critique it until it bleeds with red ink. Be merciless.

Repeat the mark-up/repair cycle as many times as you need to until you can read your paper and find no mistakes. Everything flows perfectly. The points you make send shivers down your spine. You get so wrapped up in your introduction that, even though you know what your paper is about, you can't put it down. Your conclusion brings tears to your eyes. This is how you'll know your paper is done.

The more time you spend critiquing your paper, the better it's going to be. This is why you need to give yourself plenty of time to write. If a paper is due in two weeks, start now! If you wait until the last minute, you won't be able to give your paper the time and effort it deserves. Granted, there are some kids who can write a stellar paper on the first try. If you're one of these kids, I don't even see why you bothered reading this chapter. But if you're like me, you're going to need to put a lot of time and effort into your work in order to earn a good grade. By starting a paper early, you can make sure that you have enough time to finish.

A few last points. First, some teachers allow you to turn in "drafts" early for comments. This is a great opportunity. Work on your paper to get it as polished as possible, and then see what your teacher has to say. When you get your paper back with your teacher's red marks, you know all you have to do is fix those up, and you're good to go! If you don't know if your teacher accepts drafts or not, ask.

In addition, make sure you look over your paper one last time before turning it in. Are the pages in order? Did everything print properly? Did you forget to fix one thing? Read through your paper line by line to ensure you are turning in your best work. Along with that point, don't turn in a paper that has dog-eared edges, spilt coffee on it, or any other sort of paper-blemish. If this is indeed your best work, treat it as such. This paper belongs on a pedestal, and it should look the part.

Writing can be fun, exciting, and easy. There is a basic outline to follow, and the rest stems from your creativity. In order to write well, you need to be able to read well. Whether it's analyzing a passage or text, or borrowing an author's writing style, how well you read will affect how well you write. Writing also consists of changing perspectives. Put yourself in the reader's shoes. Ask questions. Then put yourself back in the writer's role and answer those questions. Write, critique, write, critique. And that's all there is to it! Oh yeah, and have fun with it, too; writing is a great opportunity to explore your opinions and express your feelings. Enjoy it!

Chapter 4 Summary Questions

1.) When asked to comment on a passage, what are some things you can talk about?

2.) What should be included in an introduction? In a conclusion? In body paragraphs?

3.) What should you look for when revising a paper?

4.) What did you learn from this chapter that you are going to incorporate in your writing?

5

Homework Matters

It is only the ignorant who despise education.

~Publius Syrus (42 B.C.)

Shortchange your education now and you may be short of change the rest of your life.

~Unknown

Carrie was one of the most intelligent girls in my 9th grade biology class. She also had one of the worst grades. In a class where homework mattered, she didn't do it. I take that back. She actually did do her homework. She just never bothered to turn it in. Of course, this habit drove her parents and teachers crazy! I never did understand why Carrie didn't turn in her homework, but I definitely learned from her. Homework matters!

Plan Your Homework

Because some teachers place such a large emphasis on homework, it only makes sense you should also take it seriously. Make sure you write down all your homework assignments. (You don't want to let any of them slip through the cracks.) Plan ahead. Know when you have a big paper or project due, and schedule the rest of your work accordingly. For example, if you know you have a test in math on Wednesday and a paper in English due Tuesday, you might want to write the paper ahead of time and spend Monday and Tuesday preparing for the math exam. Organization and scheduling are very important skills in homework and in life.

Learn to Take Control of Your Workload Today!

In college and in the business world, it's up to you to figure out how to get all of your assignments done. Learning how to plan ahead now will help when you have three essays and four exams during the same week in college, or later in life when you have a strategic planning meeting, a budget proposal, and a major presentation to the vice president all in the same day.

Motivate Yourself

Once you figure out when you're going to do your work, you need to go ahead and do it. One way to do this is to tell yourself, "Homework first!" This motto can help motivate you to do work. You have to be your own drill-sergeant and rule-maker; forbid yourself to watch TV, hang out with friends, or play video games until your homework is done. This strategy will help you make sure you have enough time to do your work. I once knew a kid who said he didn't have enough time for his homework, because his mom made him go to bed at 10:00 p.m. When the teacher asked him when he started his homework, he said 9:15. No wonder he didn't have time!

Choosing Your Study Environment

This being said, I don't expect you not to eat or go to the bathroom because you feel like you need to get your homework done right away. As a matter of fact, if something is on your mind (like your bladder that is about to explode), you probably won't be as productive as you might otherwise be.

When studying, you need to feel comfortable. Being comfortable means not having to think about your environment. If you are thinking, "Boy, my leg is totally going to fall asleep if I keep sitting like this," or "Man, where did that paper go, I just saw it somewhere around here," your mind is not on your homework. Comfort is subjective. My friend Pete is most comfortable when he is studying on a hard wooden stool. I like to sit in an oversized squishy chair or on a sofa. My buddy Stew needs to have a big table on which to spread out his papers. Try different environments. Discover what works best for you.

Possible Study Environments

- Library
- Quiet room
- Desk
- Kitchen table
- Coffee shop
- Wooden stool
- Sofa
- Oversized chair
- Bed
- In front of a computer

Study environments can change depending on what kind of work you're doing. You should probably be at a desk or in front of a computer if you have to write a paper. However, you may try a quiet environment if you need to read.

As a rule of thumb, I usually like to study in a warm, quiet place. I like to have a snack (usually a bowl of cereal or a chocolate milk) before I start studying so that I am not concentrating on my grumbling stomach. I also like to have had just gone to the bathroom so that's not an issue.

Plan of Attack

Once you're situated, set goals for yourself. For example, look at all the homework you have and then allocate time limits for each assignment. For instance, you might come up with a schedule like this:

Plan of Attack

French............20 min.

Algebra............1 hour

English............45 min.

Biology............30 min.

From here, there are many different ways to attack the list. One possible way is to organize the list by time-to-completion, so that the homework that's estimated to take the least amount of time is at the top of the list, and the assignment that'll take the longest amount of time is at the bottom. In this case, you would do your French, then Biology, then English, and finally Algebra. Getting the easy things out of the way quickly can give you a sense of accomplishment. But there's no reason why you should organize the list by the amount of time each assignment should take. You can do the hardest stuff first and then the easiest stuff last, alphabetical order, whatever. The important thing is you have an idea of about how long your homework will take.

After having set time allocations on your homework, you can devise a reward system. If you finished your French early, relax for the remainder of the time allocated to French. If you got through French and Biology, reward yourself with a chocolate. These little prizes can help keep you motivated. You can find your own prizes—allowing yourself to munch on Milky Way bars, watch one episode of Seinfeld, or talk for half an hour on the phone to your new romantic interest—but rewarding yourself is a great way to get the homework done.

Rewarding yourself can also include taking a short break. I find I'm most productive for the first hour of work. Then, I start to get tired, things begin to look the same, and it's all downhill from there. One way to get around the monotony of homework, especially when there's a lot of it, is to always be starting anew.

For instance, in the previous example, you might try doing your French and Biology homework, and then taking a walk. That way, when you return to you studies 20 minutes later, you feel refreshed and ready to dive into your Algebra homework.

Varying your environment also helps when you have a lot of work to do. Try doing some work in a quiet atmosphere, then going to a coffee shop or another stimulating environment to do the work that doesn't require extreme focus. While you might be working the whole time, the change in scenery will help your mind stay alert and active.

Remember Why You're Doing It

Teachers usually have a reason for assigning homework. They want to solidify understanding, promote ideas, or ignite your creative talent. So when you're doing your work, ask yourself, "Why am I doing this?" and "Do I get it?" If you are learning how to conjugate verbs in Spanish, are you just copying from the example, or do you understand the principle behind it? If you are trying to find derivatives, are you looking at the back of the book for the answers, or do you know how to do it yourself? Homework is useless unless you are learning from it.

Granted, there are times when teachers assign busywork. Natasha, a girl in my Spanish class, refused to do busywork. Her grades suffered as a result. I understood where she was coming from, but I always felt that there was a reason teachers assigned busywork. On the one hand, it didn't teach me about what was going on in class, but on the other hand, it taught me a very important life lesson. In your job, or in life when you grow up, there are always mundane tasks that need to get done. If you simply refuse to do the boring parts of a job, you're going to get fired. Busywork may not be stimulating or intellectual, but it's a part of life, and the sooner you know how to buckle down and get through it, the better off you're going to be in college and in your profession.

Swallow the Big Worms First

In life, there will be tasks that have to get done, but that you REALLY don't want to do. I like to think of these tasks as worms, writhing around   in a pot labeled, "THING I DON'T WANT TO DO." If I had to eat a pot of worms, the best thing to do would be to get the biggest, fattest, juiciest worm out of the way first. From there, the next biggest worm wouldn't be as bad, and the third biggest worm would seem quite small. If something needs to get done and you don't want to do it, instead of thinking about how much you don't want to do it, it's easier to actually just do the thing you don't want to do and get it over with. After that, the next biggest thing you don't want to do won't seem that bad.

Homework is an important aspect of high school education. It deserves your attention and dedication. You need to find an appropriate place in which you study best. If you're getting tired of doing homework, try rewarding yourself or switching up your study environment. Make sure you understand what you're doing and that you're not just wasting your time. And if you're just doing busywork, recognize it, and get it done!

Chapter 5 Summary Questions

1.) What motivates you to do homework?

2.) Where do you get your best studying done? What study environments have you never tried? Do you think they could work for you?

3.) What value is there in completing an assignment early? Do you believe in doing this?

4.) What solace does the author give in regards to busywork?

6

Conquering the Exam

I was asked to memorize what I did not understand; and, my memory being so good, it refused to be insulted in that manner.

~Aleister Crowley

As I mentioned earlier, Molly was my roommate in college. Throwing the discus for Stanford, conducting independent research on arsenic contamination in Southeast Asia, and taking 20+ units each quarter, she didn't have a lot of time to study. I remember the day she had a quiz in some science class: unable to study for it the night before, she arrived to class 10 minutes early, crammed, and got an A. Molly was amazing.

What's a Study?

Unfortunately, not everyone can do that. I know I certainly can't. If you are like Molly, skip to the next chapter. But for the rest of us, there is only one way to conquer the exam: it's not fun, and it's certainly not easy; but the best remedy for test-time blues is the "Study!" My brother once asked, "Study? What's a Study? Can you eat it?" This phrase underlines the absence of studying in most high schoolers' attitudes. Here's where you learn exactly what a "Study" is and how to tackle it.

You can learn a lot in a class. So the first thing you need to do is to narrow down the spectrum of possibilities of what may be on the exam. And who better to ask than your teacher! More times than not, teachers will actually tell their students what to study. You might want to direct your questions pointedly, such as, "Does the test include the material before the midterm?" or "Are we going to be responsible for dates, or just periods?" or "Will we be asked to compare *A Separate Peace* to *A Man for All Seasons*, or should we just know the storyline behind them?" Try to be as specific in your questions as possible so you get a very clear idea of exactly what is going to be expected of you.

Conquering the Study

Once you figure out what you're supposed to study, review your notes. Sometimes it is sufficient to just read (and reread) them, but oftentimes it helps to type them up. Rewriting your notes will keep the studying real: it's hard to skim when you're writing. Some people like to make flashcards as a way to help them review the course content. I never liked the flashcard part, simply because making them always took such a long time. But for vocabulary tests, they can be a great way to test your knowledge.

One of the most important things to remember when studying is to get an early start on it. As you can see from this graph, it's important to not only get an early start on your studying, but also to continue reviewing up until the test.[iv]

CURVE OF FORGETTING

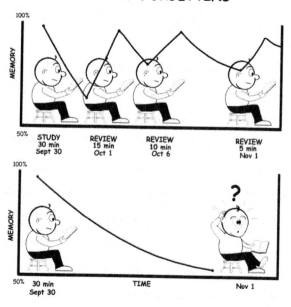

Without time pressure, you can ensure you have enough time to really learn and review the material. But how? Well, rewriting and rereading your notes is a huge start, but you're going to need to do more. Look for overarching themes and ideas. For example, in a European history course, the industrial revolution might have had a great impact on a variety of issues, so figure out how certain events can be tied back to it.

Once you figure out what some of the main themes of the test are going to be, look for examples that can illustrate the point. Oftentimes, especially in history, there are one or two themes being presented and an overflowing abundance of detail to support these ideas. Because our brains are not computers, and because we have other things we would like to be doing than just sitting around and memorizing every minute detail of a certain event, pick two or three examples that can illustrate a point. Don't worry about the rest of the details.

Now clearly this method doesn't work for tests of sheer memorization, like vocabulary or historical-dates quizzes. Some kids get worried when they realize they're going to have to memorize crazy math equations or the inner workings of photosynthesis. But memorization is easy. Picture this: you're driving down the road when that song comes on . . . you know the one . . . the new hit single that they've been playing non-stop all week. You turn up the radio and start singing along; you know all the words by heart.

If this scenario sounds at all familiar, then you have been using a memorization trick you didn't even know about. While learning the lyrics to the new hit song doesn't seem like work, the way you went about doing it can be applied to your studies. You can convert all the information you need to memorize for a test into a song. I especially like to sing math equations and historical dates. For example, I would sing something like:

> 1929 was not much fun,
> The market crashed and the depression begun.

If you're singing, learning becomes a lot more fun. Granted, my songs might never make any top-ten lists, but they do help me get through tests.

Another way to memorize data is to invent a crazy story. I was presented with a list of 16 French verbs that needed to be conjugated in the past tense with the verb *être* (to be) instead of *avoir* (to have). Looking at these verbs, I had no idea how I was going to memorize them! But then my French teacher told us this story about a man who was born in a house, who died in a house, who fell off the roof of this house . . . Well, the story wasn't amazing, but she managed to incorporate all 16 verbs into that silly story. And by repeating the story a few times, I learned those 16 verbs!

If a story is too much trouble for you, a similar technique is to take the first letter of every word and make up a crazy sentence. This technique is used in phrases like, "<u>P</u>lease <u>E</u>xcuse <u>M</u>y <u>D</u>ear <u>A</u>unt <u>S</u>ally," which is a way to remember the order of operations (Parentheses, Exponents, Multiplication, Division, Addition, Subtraction). My U.S. history teacher, Ms. Lucchesi, taught me these types of sentences work better when you relate them to sex, alcohol, and music; these topics at least make the sentences more entertaining.

Slogans are helpful: "*Gilette* (French for vest), the best for your vest," was a slogan my friend Jessica came up with when we had to memorize clothing vocabulary in French. When I was trying to remember which way the accent mark went on the word *père* (father), I told myself that it went backwards because dads can be a little backward. The bottom line is there is no limit to the crazy jargon you can think up when memorizing, and while your songs, stories, poems, slogans, and phrases might not make sense to anybody else in the world, they will help you remember what you need to memorize for the test.

Test Your Knowledge

So, how do you know when you're ready to take the test? Well, the first thing you can do is a dry run; take a practice test. Some teachers give out practice tests, and if yours does, then great! Also, sometimes textbooks have summary questions at the end of the chapters. Try answering them. If test questions are not given directly to you, then you have to be responsible for devising your own system of testing your knowledge. A great way to do this is to get together with a friend or two. Study groups are not as popular in high school as they are in college, but they are an excellent way to determine what you know and what you need to review.

Study Tips

- Reread your notes
- Rewrite your notes
- Tease out overarching themes and ideas
- Choose 2–3 illustrative examples to memorize
- Make flashcards
- Invent slogans
- Write songs to memorize information
- Create a story that is going to help you memorize facts
- Make up silly sentences in which each word stands for something (e.g. Please Excuse My Dear Aunt Sally)

Study Groups

A study group is a few people (anywhere from 2 to 5—it gets too hectic if the group gets too big) who sit around and talk about the material. A good way to prepare for a meeting is to write up questions that could be on the exam and ask them in the group. Ask the other members of the group to do the same. See how the other kids answer the questions you made up. If there is a discrepancy between the way they answered the question and the way in which you would have answered it, go back through the books and your notes to figure out who was right and why. Do the same with the questions they made up. Frequently, at least one of the questions you go over in a study group appears on the exam.

Choosing a group of kids with whom to study is very important. If you are with your closest friends, it might be more tempting to talk about the party last weekend or who you are going to take to the prom than the Biology exam you have on Tuesday. Also, you might be wasting your time if you're with a group of people who have not prepared at all for the study session and are just hoping you're going to tell them all the right answers.

I always liked to have two study groups; the first study group would be comprised of the smartest kids in the class—the kids who somehow knew every date in history off the top of their heads, or who could talk about the symbolism in Orwell's *1984* until your ears fell off. You know the ones. Anyway, I would invite two or three of these kids over to my house a day or two before the test. Of course, I would have studied on my own prior to their arrival, so that I had a strong grasp on the material and was prepared with a list of possible questions. These study sessions would be extremely helpful for me, and if there was anything we didn't understand as a group, we could ask the teacher about it the next day in class.

My second study group was made up of the best-looking men I could find: the Abercrombie-model look-a-likes, the captain of the football team, and the Homecoming King. While I didn't associate with these guys normally, they usually accepted my invitation to a study session. I have to say, these study groups were much less effective academically, simply because the majority of these guys hadn't prepared any questions, they didn't know the material, and their good looks couldn't help them memorize facts. But studying with the stud-muffins gave me a chance to explain the ideas and concepts of the class, which in turn reinforced them in my own mind.

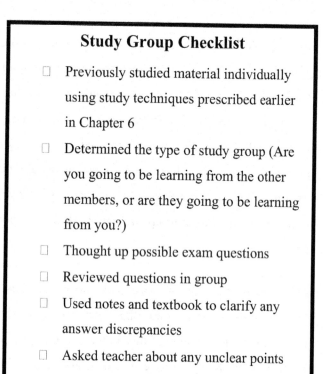

Study Group Checklist

☐ Previously studied material individually using study techniques prescribed earlier in Chapter 6

☐ Determined the type of study group (Are you going to be learning from the other members, or are they going to be learning from you?)

☐ Thought up possible exam questions

☐ Reviewed questions in group

☐ Used notes and textbook to clarify any answer discrepancies

☐ Asked teacher about any unclear points

Studying Summed Up

Up until this point, you have studied the material on your own. You asked the teacher about any points you didn't understand. You formed study groups with the smart kids (and possibly with the popular kids), and you feel like you know the material inside, outside, up, down, and in between. The night before the exam, close the books. Relax. Put on some music and luxuriate in the feeling of knowing you will succeed. Get a good night's rest. Eat a healthy breakfast. And go conquer that exam!

Chapter 6 Summary Questions

1.) What are some ideas the author suggests you do in order to memorize material?

2.) What is a study group? Have you ever formed one before? Are you excited about trying one out?

3.) What do you do in study groups? What should you do to prepare for them?

4.) What did you learn in this chapter that is going to help you prepare for your next exam?

7

Boost Your Brainpower

Education is too important to be left solely to the educators.

~Francis Keppel

I pay the schoolmaster, but it is the school boys who educate my son.

~Ralph Waldo Emerson

Formal education will make you a living; self-education will make you a fortune.

~Jim Rohn

Information Overload

I walked into the office timidly, out of place in my neat gray suit and unstable in my high heels. I took a seat at the back of the unnecessarily long conference table. Slowly, so no one would notice, I glanced at the other two interns. One seemed totally in her element: she wore her black suit as if it were her skin—you would think she had worn suits all her life. The other intern seemed to be in a state similar to mine. His blue coat contrasted sharply with his white skin, and his tie seemed to be slowly choking him. Mr. Chan walked in. He was smaller than I had imagined him, but he compensated for his height with a booming voice and a take-charge attitude. It was the first day of our internship as stock analysts in New York City, and Mr. Chan was going to make sure it was an experience we never forgot.

Bellowing in a voice over twice the decibels required, he communicated to us the rapid advances that had taken place in the financial analyst's industry. When Mr. Chan was an analyst, he had to scrounge up information from the most random and unexpected places. Today, there was an information overload, and as summer interns, it was to be our job to wade through the abundance of information that could be found on the web.

Mr. Chan, in his tailored charcoal suit and sky-blue shirt, taught me a lot more that day than just what my job would be as a summer intern. He made me realize that we are living in an era where an abundance of information is literally at our fingertips, and we can put as much or as little effort into making new discoveries as we please. There are no longer any excuses: we have all the tools necessary to expand our breadth of knowledge. The answers are out there, but it's up to us to find them.

But how do you find the answers? What are the questions? What does this story about a summer internship as a stock analyst have to do with boosting your brainpower? In order to increase your mental capacity, you first have to determine what you don't know. In your schoolwork, talking to friends or family members, even listening to the radio, pay attention. Is there a concept you didn't quite understand? Was someone's name mentioned whom you didn't recognize? If so, you've hit upon a blank spot in your knowledge. I like to think of education as a gigantic piece of Swiss cheese—a solid form with all sorts of holes in it. Learning is the process of plugging up the holes. Some holes are smaller than others—not knowing who Alice Waters is might not make or break your grade in a class. It might not even be mentioned in class. You might not ever hear that name again in your life. But . . . what if you did?

Time for Q&A

Don't be afraid to ask questions of your teachers, friends, or family. If there is any hole in your Swiss cheese, fill it up! The Internet is a great place to find answers to even the most bizarre questions. If you're over at a friend's house, and you can't remember what Beethoven's first name is, look it up! In life, you'll be constantly presented with opportunities to expand your knowledge. Use those chances to ask questions and find answers.

If, somehow, you never seem to have any questions, go out and find some. I highly recommend listening to NPR (National Public Radio) to improve your breadth of knowledge. NPR has some programs that can illustrate the gaps in your knowledge, in addition to providing you with a wide array of interesting stories and amusing facts. What do you know about Brazilian jazz? Can you talk about rent control in San Francisco apartments?

Reaching out for Knowledge

If listening to the radio doesn't suit your interests, try reading various books. Push the limits of your vocabulary. If you see a word you don't recognize, look it up and write it down, along with its meaning. Read through the vocabulary lists you make and challenge yourself to use your newfound vocabulary in everyday language.

Along with vocabulary words, try writing down quotes you like. I like to tape the quotes up on the bathroom mirror so that I can read them (over and over) while I'm brushing my teeth. While reading *Hamlet* one summer, I wrote down, "There is something rotten in the state of Denmark," because I thought it sounded like a cool quote. Later that year, I was able to incorporate that precise quote into a paper I was writing on colonialism. You never know when and where you might be able to use interesting pieces of information.

For example, I remember toiling through an article in *The New Yorker* (a magazine I highly recommend) about the former CEO of Tyco, Dennis Kozlowski. I remembered asking myself why on Earth I was reading this article—it was over 20 pages of boring facts: he had no pictures of his wife and kids on his desk, and he had purchased a duck-shaped door stopper. I didn't know who this man was (although I could have told you about his wife's 50th birthday party), and I certainly didn't care how he chose to spend his time and money. But for some reason I kept trudging through those lead-lined pages.

A year later I was at the Gramercy Tavern, one of New York's finest restaurants. I was in a group of financial hotshots, Mr. Chan included, and the conversation was as dry as the champagne they were serving. Someone mentioned Tyco and its former CEO. Suddenly, I was the star of the conversation, spouting off trivial facts about him that I had learned by reading that article. Instances like these make reading through something worthwhile. Remember, you never know when you're going to have to recall something you've read or heard on the radio, and the more tidbits of information you can draw from, the more interesting a person you are going to be.

Brain Power Boosters

- Ask questions and find answers
- Look up any name, word, or allusion you don't know
- Read everything you can get your hands on
- Write down unfamiliar vocabulary words and their definitions
- Try to incorporate your new vocabulary into your speech and writing
- Write down interesting quotes
- Listen to NPR
- Read the newspaper

Getting smart on your own isn't difficult; it just requires motivation and self-discipline. Don't be lazy! Any time you see a word, name, or allusion you aren't familiar with, look it up. Ask questions. Find answers. Read anything you can get your hands on:

The Turn of the Screw, *The New York Times*, *The Atlantic Monthly*. List vocabulary words and their definitions along with interesting quotes. Find ways to incorporate your new knowledge into your everyday life. Before you know it, you will be making allusions and references to *Candide* and quoting Winston Churchill.

Chapter 7 Summary Questions

1.) How do you know what you don't know?

2.) Explain the Swiss cheese analogy

3.) Where can you look for questions?

4.) Where can you find answers?

5.) What are you going to do to increase your brainpower?

8

Preparing for Colkge and Beyond

Anybody who accepts mediocrity—in school, on the job, in life—is a person who compromises, and when the leader compromises, the whole organization compromises.

~Charles Knight

Upon the education of the people of this country the fate of this country depends.

~Benjamin Disraeli

Asking for an "A"

"It's a whole 'nother world!" my Dad stated excitedly. "College! I never knew how to study until I got to CU Boulder." This nostalgic beginning was the preface to one of my father's favorite stories: the "Asking for an

A." All of my father's memorable stories, or at least the ones he repeats all the time, have titles. My father loved to reminisce about his college days.

"Boulder was an eye-opening experience—parties at all hours, friends dropping by at three in the morning, skiing on the weekends, hiking in Estes Park—life was so filled with social experiences that there really was no time for school work. I took organic chemistry freshman year. On the first day of class, the professor said we had to read the first three chapters of the textbook. (Hah! He can't be serious!) Then, in my freshman English class, the professor assigned us a ten-page paper due that Friday (Yah, right!), and the cost-benefit ratio for the problem sets we were supposed to do in economics just didn't seem to pay off. That's how I found myself on academic probation and forced to go to summer school.

"Breezing through the course reader, my finger settled on Colorado history. It looked easy, so I thought I would give it a try. We had a paper due every week, and since I needed to raise my GPA, I decided to actually put some work into it. Turning in what I thought to be a very decent piece of work, I decided to cover my bases and disclose my situation to the professor. I attached a note along with my paper, saying that I needed to raise my GPA, and I would really appreciate an A in the class. I felt comfortable in my seat the next Monday when the professor was handing back papers. Any reasonable human would understand my situation and act accordingly. After all, it didn't hurt the professor to give out A's, and it would make my life a heck of a lot better.

"But I was wrong. In blood red ink on the front page of my paper were carved the words, 'Mr. Curtis—you will get exactly the grade you deserve. And so far, it is an F.' I couldn't believe it! Aghast and in shock, I was determined to earn an A on my next paper. That Friday, I submitted a piece of work that would blow the prof's socks off! It came back with an ominous, overbearing red F with a neat ring around it at the top of the page.

"I continued to work that summer, and I mean really work, until I was getting A's on my weekly papers. That Colorado history class taught me what it took to get an A. And just wait until you get to college . . . I can't even describe how hard you're going to have to work to get good grades. You can't even fathom the degree of difficulty you will encounter."

Collegiate Expectations

And thus my father's "Asking for an A" story ends. You can imagine that after 18 years of hearing this story, I was petrified of going to college. I thought I would be in for the biggest shock of my life. But what came as an even bigger surprise to me than the numerous assignments and astronomical amount of reading dished out was the overall facility I had in earning A's. Now don't get me wrong; I had to work for my grades, but my experience in earning A's in college was not nearly as shockingly abrupt as my father's had been.

I attribute this disparity to two factors: the first is that after having been told how gruelingly painful the collegiate workload was going to be, I no doubt had an exaggerated image of it in mind. But the second reason, and perhaps the more pertinent one, is I had the study habits in place that allowed for a smoother transition to a more rigorous workload. I'm describing these study habits to you so, if you so choose, you too can be more prepared for college.

Places, Everyone

Chapter 1 discussed how to act in a classroom setting. Granted, in a lecture hall, your tactics might have to be slightly altered. But the general rules still apply. If you're used to sitting in the front of a classroom, positioning yourself in the front of a lecture hall is not going to seem like an out-of-body experience. Sitting in the front of a lecture hall makes the size of the class seem less intimidating—you don't see the 543 other kids behind you. Being in the front makes the hall more like a classroom, a setting you may be more used to.

Making your presence known to the professor in college might be more challenging than in high school. With hundreds of other students staring at them, professors might not notice eye-contact as much as high school teachers. However, asking questions, engaging the professor, and nodding your head when you understand a concept will red-flag you as a student who really cares.

Take Note

Note taking is an essential part of any college student's academic life. Get the experience taking notes in high school so you learn what useful notes are and what's unnecessary. I knew a freshman at Stanford University who was constantly scribbling notes. She would write so quickly that sparks would occasionally ignite from the friction created between the paper and the tip of her pencil. I once sat beside this arduous note-taker. The professor had hardly addressed the class, and her pencil was already in motion. I leaned over and let my eyes wonder onto her paper. I couldn't imagine what she could possibly be writing. "Good morning! Can everybody hear me? The microphone doesn't seem to be working so well today." This was a class on Race and Ethnicity, not how to be a scribe in a courtroom. I was astounded. The girl was so busy writing down useless information that she could potentially miss important points. Get used to taking notes in high school, so you can feel comfortable writing the essentials down in your college lectures.

Preparation and Organization

Chapter 1 also discussed the necessity of coming to class prepared. This rule continues to hold true in college, but the degree of preparedness might vary somewhat. For example, in high school you want to make sure you have paper, a pencil, and your homework and textbooks. In college, these are the minimum requirements, but in order to stand out, you might have to do more. Bring in articles from *The New York Times* relating to America's foreign policy in the Middle East for your contemporary political science class. Peruse the web for information that complements or contradicts your professor's viewpoints. Do background research to better understand the concepts of the class.

Chapter 1 also went over the importance of organization in your locker, your binder, and your planner. In college you're not going to have a desk or a locker, but the ability for you to organize your schedule is going to be of utmost importance. With Midnight-Soccer matches every Monday, Toga parties on Wednesday nights, and Thirsty Thursdays, managing your workload becomes a great challenge.

If you start keeping a planner in high school and know what is due when, you'll be a lot better off in college.

Dealing with Profs.

Chapter 2 discussed how to deal with teachers. Professors are similar creatures, but you may or may not have the ability to establish close rapports with them, depending on the type of school in which you decide to matriculate. If you refine your skills in high school and know how to converse with teachers without looking like you're sucking up, you're going to get along better with college professors. Also, in college, asking for extra help or attending office hours is a regular practice. If you're used to discussing the material with teachers outside of class, and if you know how to come to a meeting prepared with notes and questions, your time is going to be spent much more effectively.

In high school you might have met some truly amazing teachers. If you're open to getting to know teachers for who they are and for what they believe in, you're going to learn some incredible things. For instance, my French teacher in high school once told me I shouldn't sacrifice any of my ideals and ambitions when I got a boyfriend, because I would end up resenting him for it. (Hardly a subject that most high school French teachers cover—I was a little surprised myself!) At the time, I had no idea what she was talking about, but as I grew up, her words made more and more sense. Teachers can present us with insightful pearls of wisdom if we are open to new ideas. In college, your professors are most likely going to have even more mind-boggling thoughts they will be willing to share with you. If you're open to the idea of learning outside the classroom, you'll be greatly rewarded.

Book Worms

Chapter 3 outlined how to read a book. If you read like this in high school, you're going to have no problem reading in college. The only challenge you'll face is not having enough time to get all your reading done. But if you're looking to understand the material, you have the skills to do it. Marking the pages and taking notes in the margins will enable you to look back on the text and pinpoint exact phrases or ambiguities you might want to bring up in a discussion session or in office hours. Writing summaries at the end of every chapter will make it much easier for you to study for a test, write a term paper, or find a particular quote.

An Essay for All Topics

Much like reading, writing assignments will be much easier in college if you understand how to go about writing a paper. Sure, assignments and professors differ, so what works for one might not cut it for another. But you are at such an advantage! You get to try out your writing technique in high school before having to prove yourself in the collegiate setting. In some college classes there is neither a mid-term nor a final exam. Grades rest solely on a final paper. In a scenario like this, wouldn't you like to know how to write a paper? Start practicing now! Use the structure outlined in Chapter 4, and see what kind of feedback you get from your high school teachers.

Homework Matters

Chapter 5 pertained to the importance of homework. In college, depending on what kind of classes you take and what kind of school you go to, homework may or may not contribute to part of your final grade. But that doesn't mean that you shouldn't do it. In fact, in many cases, homework is a way for you to gauge what you know. For example, every week in my Spanish class we had to complete a minimum of three exercises in our workbooks. While there were hundreds of exercises, students usually knew if they understood a concept or not after doing three. If you do the three exercises and still don't understand the difference between *ser* ("to be") and *estar* (also "to be"), you might try doing more exercises or setting up an appointment with the professor.

Too many times I have heard college students say they are not going to do their homework because it doesn't count. What they don't understand is it does count! If you don't do your homework, how can you possibly know if you really understand the material or not? Because you'll have attached a strong value to homework in high school, it's unlikely you'll fall into the habit of neglecting homework assignments in college.

The "Study," Still Kickin'

Not only will you be in the habit of doing homework, but you also will know what kind of study environments work best for you. Because you've explored these options in high school, you might know right off the bat that you have to get out of your room and go straight to the library if you want to write an essay on Shakespeare's *The Tempest*.

Conversely, you might also know listening to Bach's "Minuet in G" when you are writing up a lab report is soothing and beneficial. But just because you know what study environments work well for you, don't be afraid to explore others. I found freshman year I could do an inordinate amount of work in the laundry room. Sophomore year I found a little cubby, cleverly named "69," where I went when I needed to be extremely productive. Both places were quiet environments, and I learned I studied best in quiet places when I was in high school.

Testing Times

Finally, studying for a college test is going to be a lot easier when you know how to study. Being comfortable with study groups is key, because in college study groups are vastly popular. Extracting the essence of a particular class, summarizing important points, and choosing illustrative examples are going to get you far. Having notes to reread, both in your notebook and in the margins of your books, is going to be a huge bonus. The great news is you will have your high school career to refine these techniques so by the time you get to college, you will have a smooth transition.

The Real World

But wait! There's more good news! These study habits pay off even after you graduate from college. Whether you're applying for a job or building a resume, the study skills you have learned and used will be of great benefit to you. First of all, you can tell an interviewer you are self-motivated. Reading a book, taking notes in the margins, and then writing summaries at the end of every chapter isn't easy, but you did it, and it paid off grade-wise. Now it will pay off in the real world.

In addition to being self-motivated, you can also demonstrate your ability to be responsible, accountable, and organized. Making sure you arrive to class on time translates into being prepared for business meetings. Completing all your homework on time is comparable to meeting deadlines and accepting responsibility. Keeping track of all your assignments and turning in neat work shows you can multi-task and gives your work a professional touch.

Qualities from Studying

- Self-motivated
- Accountable
- Able to multi-task
- Responsible
- Organized
- Professional

Besides providing you with various skills, these study habits can teach you about yourself and how you work. Do you work better in groups or alone? Do you prefer a quiet or stimulating environment? Do you perform your best work in the morning or in the evening? You can use what you know about yourself and how you work to narrow down the right job for you.

Who's the Boss?

Once you obtain a job, you're probably going to find yourself with a boss. Establishing rapports with your teachers can be like getting to know your boss. It's quite common to find employees who fear their boss. They remind me of kindergarteners who run the other way screaming when the principal walks down the hall. A charming, friendly bookkeeper I knew always shivered and became stiff when the boss walked by. A witty secretary transformed into a groveling head-nodder whenever she spoke to her superior. It doesn't have to be that way!

Bosses, just like teachers, are real people. Although they might seem demanding or unfeeling, they have wants and needs similar to our own. Just like teachers, they should be treated with respect, though not with back-bending reverence. Get to know your boss—perhaps he is an art collector—maybe she skis on the weekends—perhaps he has a two-year old daughter. Learn from your boss. Just as you might sit in office hours with a teacher, spend time (perhaps a lunch) with your boss to get to know her better. She in turn will get to know you better. Only good things can come of that.

Finally, in a work setting, you might have to conform to your boss's demands. Do you remember how some teachers dream of students who want to learn? Remember how we discussed becoming that student? Believe it or not, bosses might have similar hopes and dreams. Perhaps they would like an employee who gets the job done. Maybe they are looking for someone who doesn't need to be told what to do. They could even possess an underlying desire to have an employee who smiles. Learning to read your teachers and what makes them happy will help you when you're dealing with your boss. And this, in turn, could augment your salary, speed up your promotion, and enrich your overall status in the company.

Studying, Summed Up

The study skills outlined in this book will help you improve your grades in high school. But they can do so much more than this. They can make the transition into college smoother because you'll already know how to study. Office hours, study groups, and lecture halls won't faze you. These study skills can also improve your resume and provide you with illustrative examples of your ability to demonstrate responsibility, accountability, and organization. Furthermore, they can assist you when you get a job, because you can treat your boss just like one of your teachers. Figuring out what your boss is looking for in an employee could help your status in the company, and getting to know your boss a little better might be both useful and interesting. And think—all of this from some simple study habits!

Chapter 8 Summary Questions

1.) How does sitting in the front of a classroom in high school affect your transition to college?

2.) How might you prepare differently for a college course, versus a high school class?

3.) How is establishing a relationship with a professor or a boss like creating a rapport with a high school teacher? How is it different?

4.) What is the most valuable piece of advice you have learned in this book? What is going to help you as you move on to college or when you get a job?

9

Study Skill Swap

It's not what you know. It's not who you know. It's what who you know knows.

~Btanen

There are two rules for success in life:
1. Don't tell people everything you know.

~Anon.

The techniques and philosophies outlined in this book have helped me get through school, but I certainly don't hold the monopoly on study habits. Here are a few skills that various Stanford students suggest:

Matthew Gamboa:

"I'm a sophomore here at Stanford University, who is about ready to join a neurobiology lab. One of the most frequent problems I remember hearing about from other kids when I was in high school was a poor mindset from the start. Students would think about what work they would have to do, say, for a given night, and focus on either how much they didn't like the material or how badly they perceived their skills to be in it. My first tip is to take a step back from actually studying. Ask yourself, why am I studying this? What is the goal? Am I interested in the material, or do I need to do well in the course to attain some other goal. Once the goal is established, if you have a tendency not to like the material, remind yourself that it is a task that it is in your best interest to complete, given the goals you have just reminded yourself of.

"Other than that, my general suggestion is to monitor your thoughts every once in a while. Be mindful of either wandering thoughts or of continual thoughts of displeasure coming directly from the task at hand. Again, the idea is to stop negative thought patterns before they become disruptive, replacing them with positive feedback, i.e., the attainment of a given goal."

Stephanie Adams:

"As a visual/hands-on learner, the best study tool I use is drawing. I have a collection of colored pens and markers that I use specifically as study tools. This works best for subjects that require a mechanistic understanding rather than memorization. In biology, drawing can be tremendously helpful. Not only do I make pretty, colorful notes that are fun to look over later, but in the process of drawing them I usually am able to solidify my conceptual understanding of the material. (Side note: I didn't discover that I was a visual learner until I did very badly in a science class and realized I wasn't studying right. The next quarter my grade went up one full letter, and I owe that all to turning studying into art.)

"Other recommended tips: Use the Internet (with caution, of course) to find other sources of information if an assigned reading or textbook is confusing or incomplete. FLASHCARDS are wonderful. And here is a key one: Explain to friends/family about what you are learning; this helps you realize what you do and don't understand."

Edward Boenig:

"I recommend:

- "A small sleep debt; have you taken Dr. Dement's class on Sleep and Dreams or heard of it?
- "A comfortable place to study, specifically with a book stand so that you're not hunched over for hours.
- "Free-writing a summary and analysis of what I read right after I read."

Molly Meyer:

"I approach school with a very active perspective. When I sit in class, I maintain good posture, and I lock my eyes onto the teacher and/or visual aids throughout the class period. Interestingly, my grade school teachers told my parents at teacher-parent conferences that my attention was so focused that I was burning holes through them with my eyes and that I was like a sponge, absorbing everything that they taught.

"As I have continued in school, those innate tendencies for intense focus have come into my conscious academic habits. And now I turn on/off my 'super power' of focus to minimize my study time and maximize my time doing more fun things! If I learn the material when I hear it in class, then my study time can be a simple and quick review—rather than a teaching session.

"In addition to my active focus, I know that I am a very physical learner. I have trained myself in sports for my whole life, so to remember more information, it is best for me to use those strengths to my advantage when learning other things. When reviewing for a test, I pace and stretch as I read my notes. When I am writing a paper, I squat rather than sit at my desk, or I get in crazy yoga positions while typing at the computer. Also, when preparing for 20-minute to 2-hour presentations, I can't (and don't want to) memorize a whole script. Instead, after I prepare and practice several times, I give the presentation to myself while I am on a long bike ride. This helps me get the information ingrained in my head because of my physical learning style.

"Also, when giving a presentation, my body is experiencing stress, which can manifest physically as cold clammy hands, sweating armpits, dry mouth, and restricted breathing. Just as in sports, its best to practice as closely to my competition scenario as possible—the same holds for academics. If you sweat when giving presentations, then sweat when you practice it!"

Will McLennen:

"Talk to your teachers/profs often, and get a good night's sleep."

Kent Anderson:

"For math, science, and engineering classes, I try to summarize all my notes and the book in 1–2 pages (key formulas, definitions, equations, etc). Then it's nothing but practicing problems and taking old exams. The first time I allow myself to use the sheet, by the end I don't. And to keep from stressing too much, it's nice to bake cookies and convince people to take a study break."

Marisa Macias:

"My advice for studying effectively:

- "Create a study space. It's easy to be working, become distracted by a bill due in three days, and get carried away taking care of that. Putting away letters, magazines, etc., makes your work area only about studying.

- "Earplugs! If someone is having a conversation outside your door, or listening to music, or watching TV, it's easy to get caught up in it. Low decibel earplugs can deafen you just a little bit more so that other people's noise is less distracting, but if the phone rings or someone needs to talk to you, you can still hear it.

- "Supposedly you only are effective about 60% of the time—don't plan every minute of every day, leave room for unexpected things (it's grandma's birthday, I have to call her) so that you don't get too far behind.

- "For papers, I often make a list of all the most pertinent quotes from the text—usually moving them around into a cohesive order and looking at them collectively gives me a sense of structure for the paper."

Wendy Goldberg:

"When writing an essay, highlight the topic sentence of each paragraph to create a mini-outline of your essay."

Allison Campbell:

"I used to think that flash cards were only for learning addition in elementary school, but I've found that they're the best way to learn. I'm going off to med school in the fall and plan to bring a huge supply of index cards!!!"

Emily Neaville:

Studying for tests:

"When I first got to college, I really had no idea how to study. I remember being shocked by my very first C in a class—it didn't occur to me that I needed some sort of *plan* to do well on the exams. Since then, I've developed some tricks that help me study for exams. The most useful of these works for exams with a lot of memorization and is very simple but powerful. Let's say you're faced with 6 chapters to study (it helps to read them first!) Go through each chapter *quickly* and copy down all the important concepts and facts on a sheet of paper or two. Usually you don't have a lot of time, but you're just skimming and writing down a few words to jog your memory. Do the same for all the chapters, but keep each chapter on a separate sheet of paper; you remember things better if they're grouped together the way you learned them. If there are things you don't understand, you can circle them, highlight them, or recopy them onto yet another sheet of paper, but don't worry about them yet.

"Next, go through your notes and handouts from class and do the same. By the end of this, you should have created a set of study guides that list everything *you* think you need to know for the exam, and in the process, you've probably learned about half of it. Now you can review your sheets instead of the pile of books and notes, and studying suddenly seems a lot more manageable!

Talking with professors:

"To a freshman (and to many seniors!), professors seem unapproachable. Maybe they're busy, or maybe you feel like your questions are stupid. I just have a little advice: don't worry about it! Most professors will be excited that you are interested in their topic (unfortunately this is not a hard and fast rule, especially in a research university, but it does apply to *most*).

"In addition, don't forget that they're human too, and they are concerned that you learn and have a good experience in your class. This means that not only is it OK to approach them, but you *should* approach them. If you're not doing well in the class, talk to your professor—he/she might be able to suggest a different way of studying, or an extra project you can do. If you're doing well in the class and are interested in where to learn more, ask—if you develop a strong relationship with your professor based on mutual interest, he/she can give you a lot in return—think advising, recommendations, etc."

Jess Lang:

- "Anything you write yourself helps. Flashcards, recopying notes, etc. Just the process of writing material out helps you remember it better.

- "Don't force yourself too much. Everyone needs a break after awhile. The more you push yourself, the more tired you and your brain will become, and the less productive you will be. So, at least once every two hours, try [to] take a break for about 15–20 minutes. Watch some TV, sit around and relax, or go out and get some fresh air, walk a bit to clear your head and get your blood moving. Then you can go back to work revitalized, and with new energy.

- 'Try and keep yourself interested. Boredom slows you down. I try to change subjects every 30–60 minutes, depending on the work I am doing. After a half an hour of reading, I generally tend to get restless, so at that point I change to something else—homework in another subject, or just another task/project I have to do in order to have a change of scene. By not staying with anything for too long, you get bored less and stay more productive.

- "When working on a research paper, it is handy to keep note-cards of useful quotes. You write the quote on the center of the card, along with any comments about its significance with regards to your paper, a title on the top line that is a one to two word summary of the quote or what is important about the quote, and then write the author and page number on the bottom right to keep track of it. Then, when making an outline later, or just going through quotes to use in the paper, you do not have to flip through books to find them. You can reference them quickly using the card titles. Another advantage of this is that writing the quotes out helps you remember them better for further use, and writing notes about it/writing a card title forces you to analyze the quote and summarize the quote in your own words, encouraging deeper understanding of the material.

"If you are really into organization, you can color code your cards (either with colored cards, or by taking white note-cards and drawing a line along the top with

164

a highlighter)—each color can correspond to either a different source (book, article, interview, etc.) or to a different topic (this would help with quote categorization and facilitate outline-writing).

"Other than that, I think all of my study tips are common sense—procrastination is bad, pacing is good, stressing out is counterproductive (wastes time in which you could be working, and just works you up so that you can't be as productive), explaining concepts to other people enhances your own understanding of concepts as well as your memory for the concept, etc."

Michael Zakaras:

"I am a senior at Stanford and am majoring in history. I write for the *Stanford Progressive* and just finished an honors thesis on the history of California wine. I have found that teaching others is one of the most effective ways to learn because it forces you to master the material. In high school, I used to do my math problems on a white board in front of a parent or a friend. I also liked to brainstorm and discuss paper topics with someone.

"I find that when writing a paper, brainstorming and outlining are critical. I never just sit down and write because I get two pages into a paper, just to find myself totally lost in a sea of unchained thoughts. To avoid writer's block, I construct an outline to get a clear idea of where the paper is going before I even start writing."

Andy Clavin:

"My biggest study tip is to avoid procrastination. That being said, I have a few other study habits. If I can't concentrate at night, I go to sleep and wake up in the morning for a fresh start. I like to go to bed early before a test, and cram a little bit before the exam."

LaCona Woltmon:

"I like to review my notes before I go to bed. When studying for a mid-term or a final, I find it extremely helpful to make cheat-sheets for myself. I do this by going through my notes and writing down the most important points. The process of teasing out the essential information is extremely beneficial in reviewing, and having a simple cheat-sheet makes

studying less intimidating. Also, I highly recommend
you take notes in your books."

Chapter 9 Summary Questions

1.) List three suggestions these Stanford students made that coincided with ones the author put forth.

2.) List three suggestions these Stanford students made that the author didn't touch on previously in the book.

3.) What were the three most helpful pieces of advice?

4.) How are you going to incorporate them into your study habits?

Notes

[i] Sekhri-Feachem, Neelam, Prashant Yadav, Kirsten Curtis. "'Barriers to access: An assessment of stakeholder risks and incentives in the value chain for Artemisinin Combination Therapy (ACT) treatments. ' MIT-Zaragoza International Logistics Institute, 2007.

[ii] Ibid.

[iii] Trimble, John. Writing with Style, Prentice Hall, 2000.

[iv] Physiological Factors in Influencing Learning, University of Bozeman, Montana.

CPSIA information can be obtained
at www.ICGtesting.com
Printed in the USA
BVOW10s1952180517
484527BV00007B/114/P